That Summer—That Fall

&

Far Rockaway

That Summer—That Fall

&

Far Rockaway

FRANK D. <u>GILROY</u>

Random House · New York

To Blanche

Foreword

It was my intention that *That Summer—That Fall* should work both realistically and as ritual. Unfortunately, the latter element has, so far, escaped detection, and the play is taken as further evidence of my exclusive dedication to the "real."

Actually, my ambitions are considerably more catholic, and I include *Far Rockaway* in this volume to demonstrate the point.

F.D.G.

THAT SUMMER—THAT FALL *was first presented by Edgar Lansbury at the Helen Hayes Theatre in New York City, on March 16, 1967, with the following cast:*

(*In order of appearance*)

ANGELINA CAPUANO	Irene Papas
STEVE FLYNN	Jon Voight
ZIA FILOMENA	Elena Karam
JOSEPHINE MARINO	Tyne Daly
VICTOR CAPUANO	Richard Castellano

Directed by Ulu Grosbard
Settings and lighting by Jo Mielziner
Costumes by Theoni V. Aldredge
Music composed and conducted by David Amram

SYNOPSIS OF SCENES

ACT ONE

SCENE 1: Part of a playground in lower Manhattan.
SCENE 2: The Capuanos' apartment.
SCENE 3: Three A.M. the next morning.
SCENE 4: Afternoon, one week later.
SCENE 5: The next morning, 11 A.M.
SCENE 6: Five P.M. the same day.
SCENE 7: Midnight, several days later.
SCENE 8: Several nights later.

ACT TWO

SCENE 1: Eight P.M., the night of the dance.
SCENE 2: Three hours later.
SCENE 3: The next morning.
SCENE 4: Late that night.
SCENE 5: The playground.

That Summer—That Fall

Act One

Act One

The setting is part of a playground in lower Manhattan, including a handball court and two benches. The time is mid-morning, a warm day in August. As the house lights dim, we hear the rhythmic bounce of a ball.

As the curtain rises we see a young man in his early twenties, dressed in a T-shirt, playing handball. Well built, handsome in a winning boyish way, he hits the ball in desultory fashion—as though he were preoccupied, killing time.

Seated on one of the benches bordering the court, reading a book, is ANGELINA CAPUANO. *She is thirty-six, an attractive woman whose severely arranged hair and matronly dress make her appear prim and older than she is. Head bowed, absorbed in her book, she seems oblivious to the young man's presence.*

He interrupts a volley to look at his wrist watch, then crosses to a second bench over which are draped a jacket and a knapsack. He dons the jacket, shoulders the knapsack, goes offstage.

As the sound of his steps recede, ANGELINA *lifts her head, rises, and looks after him. As she looks, her right hand moves slowly to her mouth—as though to stifle an utterance.*

Lights down

SCENE 2

The setting is now the Capuanos' *apartment, in an Italian neighborhood in lower Manhattan.*
The stage is divided between the living room and VICTOR *and* ANGELINA's *bedroom. A hallway (visible when required) links these rooms and offers the door to* ZIA's *room. Upstage in the living room is an opening that gives access to the rest of the apartment and the entrance door, which is offstage.*
The furnishings, expensive, in good repair, contrast with the building, which is old and worn. Religious pictures and relics are in evidence.
The time is afternoon, the same day.
As the lights come up, ANGELINA *sits in a rocker in the living room; she rocks in a way that denotes agitation. The source of her discomfort seems to be an open window and the sounds* (children's voices *predominate*) *emanating from it.*
Across the room, knitting, apparently oblivious to ANGELINA's *mounting irritation, is her aunt* ZIA FILOMENA, *in her late fifties.*
A chorus of shouts prompts ANGELINA *to go to the window; she slams it shut.* ZIA *regards her.*

ANGELINA   I wish they never built that playground.

ZIA   There was a breeze.

ANGELINA   I have a headache. (ZIA *resumes her knitting.*
ANGELINA *rocks a bit more; then she stops*) Maybe we'll go away for a couple of weeks—to the shore.

6

ZIA He won't take the time.

ANGELINA You and I.

ZIA I don't like the shore.

ANGELINA The mountains then.

ZIA We'll see.

ANGELINA That means no.

ZIA Go yourself.

ANGELINA Sure.

ZIA What do you care what a bunch of old ladies say?

ANGELINA (*In Italian, sharply*) Smettila! (*ZIA glances at her, then returns to her knitting*) I'm sorry.

ZIA It's all right.

ANGELINA I didn't sleep well.

ZIA It's the heat. (*The doorbell rings*) Stay.
     (*She rises; goes off; returns with* JOSIE (JOSEPHINE MARINO), *a pretty, vivacious girl of eighteen*)

JOSIE (*To* ANGELINA) How about a wash and set?

ANGELINA I don't know.

JOSIE You could use it.

ANGELINA Thanks.

ZIA You were complaining about your hair.

ANGELINA (*To* JOSIE) . . . All right.
(JOSIE's *attention is drawn to the entrance of* VICTOR
CAPUANO, *a large, barrel-chested man, in his mid-
fifties. Well groomed, manicured nails, custom-made
suit, he exudes an air of prosperity, self-satisfaction,
and authority. At the moment he is exceedingly disturbed and trying unsuccessfully not to show it*)

JOSIE Hi, Victor.

VICTOR Josie.

ANGELINA What brings *you* home?

VICTOR (*To* JOSIE) Would you excuse us?

JOSIE Sure. (*To* ANGELINA) I'll get my things.
(*She exits*)

ANGELINA (*To* VICTOR) What is it? (VICTOR, *his agitation
mounting, listens for the sound of the front door closing
after* JOSIE; *he mops his forehead*) What's wrong?

8

VICTOR Nothing. (ZIA *blesses herself*) There's nothing wrong.

ANGELINA Say it . . . Go on.

VICTOR . . . Before we were married I told you about a woman I went with . . . Irish.

ZIA God help us.

VICTOR Don't start.

ANGELINA You heard from her . . . ? Well?

VICTOR From the child—a boy . . . He came to the restaurant.

ZIA (*Sarcastically*) Nothing's wrong.

VICTOR "My name is Steve Flynn. I think I'm your son." Just like that.

ZIA What's he want?

VICTOR Nice-looking. From California. Goes to college.

ZIA What does he want?

VICTOR Nothing.

ANGELINA Why's he here?

VICTOR I'm the father!

ZIA Tell the world.

ANGELINA How come he waited so long?

VICTOR Lilly never told him about me. He was going through some things she left—found papers.

ANGELINA Left?

VICTOR She's dead.

ANGELINA . . . Where is he?

VICTOR Downstairs.

ANGELINA Tell him to come up.

VICTOR It's his first trip East.

ANGELINA Bring him up.

VICTOR He doesn't know anybody in New York.

ANGELINA . . . You invited him to stay here.

VICTOR   What could I do?

ZIA   Leave it to you.

ANGELINA   How long?

VICTOR   The end of the summer—three weeks.

ANGELINA   . . . All right.

VICTOR   What could I do?

ANGELINA   I said all right.

VICTOR (*To* ZIA)   What could I do? (*He goes to a window fronting the street and calls down*) Steve . . . Two B. (*To* ANGELINA *and* ZIA) He hitchhiked across the country—got everything he owns in one of those canvas bags like soldiers carry.

ANGELINA   A knapsack?

VICTOR   Yeah. (ANGELINA *turns away*) Very polite—kept calling me "sir." I—

ANGELINA (*Maintaining her back to him*)   —Victor.

VICTOR   Yeah?

ANGELINA I've changed my mind: Say there's no room—give him money for a hotel.

VICTOR Why?

ZIA . . . The neighbors.

VICTOR What do I care about the neighbors?
(*There is a knock at the door.* VICTOR *goes off*)

ZIA (*To* ANGELINA) You should have said no in the beginning.
(ANGELINA *exits into the kitchen.* VICTOR *returns with* STEVE—*the young man we saw in the playground*)

VICTOR (*To* STEVE, *indicating* ZIA) My wife's aunt. (*To* ZIA) This is Steve.

STEVE Pleased to meet you.
(ZIA *nods*)

VICTOR Aunt, in Italian, is *zia*. That's what we call her.

ZIA (*To* STEVE) Do you travel one road or two?

STEVE Pardon me?

ZIA Do you travel one road or two?
(STEVE, *puzzled, turns to* VICTOR *for explanation*)

VICTOR She was born with a caul, tells fortunes—like the gypsies. Treat her nice or she'll stick pins in your doll.

ZIA Don't ridicule when you don't understand!

VICTOR Give him a break—he just got here. (*Calling*) Angy . . . *Angy*. (ANGELINA *appears*) I'd like you to meet Steve.

STEVE How do you do?
  (*She just looks at him*)

VICTOR I figured he'd use the back room.

ANGELINA Yes.

STEVE (*To* ANGELINA) You're sure I'm not putting you out?

VICTOR Positive. Zia'll show you the way. (STEVE *follows* ZIA *off. To* ANGELINA) I don't like it any more than you do, but he's here—let's make the best of it.

ANGELINA What do we do with him for three weeks?

VICTOR Show him the sights.

ANGELINA I thought you were so busy.

VICTOR *You* can take him.

13

ANGELINA No!

(ZIA *and* STEVE, *minus his knapsack, return*)

STEVE It's a nice room.

VICTOR Kind of small.

STEVE You should see some of the places I've been staying.

VICTOR Sit. (STEVE *sits. To* ANGELINA) He hitchhiked across the country. (*This elicits no response from her. He returns his attention to* STEVE) How long did it take?

STEVE Two weeks.

VICTOR I always wanted to do that—cross the country. But not hitchhiking. (*He forces a laugh.* STEVE *smiles politely. The women's expressions are unchanged*) Maybe you'd like to take a rest or something.

STEVE No.

VICTOR Sure?

STEVE Positive.

VICTOR Hungry?

STEVE No.

VICTOR Coffee maybe?

STEVE No, thanks.
(*Silence ensues until* VICTOR *can't bear it*)

VICTOR A lot of people wonder why we still live here. For
one thing, it's near the restaurant—besides, I own the
building . . . (*No response.* VICTOR *turns to* ANGELINA
and ZIA: *he indicates* STEVE) Nice-looking, huh? (*To*
STEVE) Like they say, it don't come from the sticks and
stones. (VICTOR *starts to laugh—stops when he sees that
no one else finds it funny; he mops his forehead*) Some
weather you picked—hottest summer in years. But then
you're used to it . . . California.

STEVE Yes.
(*Silence*)

VICTOR (*Rising*) I'm going to get a glass of water. Anyone
else?

STEVE No, thanks. (VICTOR *exits into the kitchen.* STEVE
glances at ZIA, *who regards him uninterruptedly. Uncom-
fortable, he looks away; he tries to make conversation. To*
ANGELINA) It's very nice of you. (*She looks at him uncomprehendingly*) To put me up. (*She offers no reaction,
and turns away. He tries again*) Were you in the playground this morning?

ANGELINA What?

STEVE I was waiting for the restaurant to open. I went to
the playground. I think I saw you sitting on a bench by
the handball court.

ZIA You were there?

ANGELINA Did I say I wasn't? You've got a good memory. (VICTOR *enters with a glass of water*)

VICTOR There's all kinds of things to do in New York: shows, sports, museums, concerts—anything.

STEVE I'd like to try all of them. (*Silence*)

VICTOR (*Rising. He speaks to* STEVE) Well, you'll have to excuse me.

ANGELINA Why?

VICTOR (*To* STEVE) We're shorthanded at the restaurant.

STEVE Can you use a busboy?

ANGELINA You know how?

STEVE Yes.

ANGELINA (*To* VICTOR) There you go.

VICTOR He's here for a vacation.

STEVE I'd enjoy it.

16

VICTOR It's hard work.

STEVE I'm used to that.

ANGELINA (*To* VICTOR) What can you lose?

VICTOR I'm a tough boss.

STEVE I'll take my chances.

ANGELINA Well?

VICTOR . . . Okay.

ZIA What do we tell people? (*They turn to her, uncomprehending*) When they ask who he is.

VICTOR To mind their own business!

STEVE Why not tell them the truth? (*They regard him apprehensively*) That I'm the son of an old friend. (*It takes a moment, until he smiles, to realize he's offering them a graceful way out*)

VICTOR (*Laughing, but still taken aback by the audacity of the joke*) That's it—the son of an old friend. (*To* STEVE) Come on.

STEVE (*To* ANGELINA) Thanks.
    (*He follows* VICTOR *out*)

ZIA You should have said no—right away.

ANGELINA It's only three weeks.
> (JOSIE, *with her hairsetting equipment, enters, looking back to the door*)

JOSIE Who was *that?*

ZIA With Victor?

JOSIE Uh-huh.

ZIA The son of an old friend.

JOSIE Wow!

ZIA He's staying with us.

JOSIE Hurray for our side.

ZIA Till the end of the month—three weeks.

JOSIE I'll have to work fast.

ANGELINA I've changed my mind.

JOSIE This may not be such a bad summer after all.

ANGELINA I've changed my mind . . . (JOSIE *regards her*)
My hair's all right.

18

JOSIE   I was going to do it different.

ANGELINA   No.

JOSIE   Just a set.

ANGELINA   Nothing!
   (ANGELINA *turns away.* JOSIE *is perplexed.* ZIA
   ushers JOSIE *off.* ANGELINA *remains as she is*)

Lights Down

It is three A.M. *the next morning.*
As the lights come up, there is a single light on in the
living room. The stage is deserted.
We hear the outside door open; VICTOR *and* STEVE *enter.*

VICTOR   Tired?

STEVE   I won't have any trouble sleeping.

VICTOR   I warned you.

STEVE   True.

VICTOR (*Pouring himself a glass of wine*) Want something
to drink or eat?

STEVE   No.

VICTOR   No bad habits, huh? (STEVE *smiles*) You're a good
worker.

STEVE   Thanks.

VICTOR   I think I'll promote you. (STEVE *regards him ques-*
tioningly) You'll relieve me a few hours a day—show
people to their tables, and like that.

STEVE   I don't have a suit.

VICTOR My tailor'll fix you up. (*He looks for a reaction.* STEVE *offers none*) You don't like that?

STEVE No.

VICTOR You don't want to be obligated to me.

STEVE To anyone.

VICTOR Good for you . . . How about if I take the suit out of your pay?

STEVE Pay?

VICTOR Don't thank me until you see how much . . . Well?

STEVE The way you worked me tonight, it better be pretty substantial.

VICTOR If you're not satisfied you can always quit.

STEVE Fair enough.

VICTOR And if I'm not satisfied I'll fire you.

STEVE You've got a deal.

VICTOR (*Finishes his drink, then rises*) . . . Well, I guess I'll turn in. Good-night.

STEVE Good-night.

VICTOR You change your mind about something to eat—
help yourself.

STEVE Thanks.
(VICTOR *starts from the room; he stops and turns*)

VICTOR Your mother and me went together over a year.
Had a lot of good times, but it didn't take. We said all
the good-byes—then she found out she was expecting.
I was willing to do the right thing, but she disappeared.
I tried to find her. Hired detectives. (*He extracts a packet
of papers from his pocket*) It's all here. (*He drops the
packet on a coffee table*) Good-night.

STEVE Good-night.
(VICTOR *exits.* STEVE *removes the rubber band hold-
ing the packet; he starts to read the contents.* VICTOR
*enters the bedroom, turns on a light, starts to un-
dress.* ANGELINA *sits up in bed; she regards him*)

ANGELINA Well?

VICTOR Good worker . . . *been* working since he was
twelve.

ANGELINA . . . That's all?

VICTOR His mother's mother was Swedish . . . The
blonde hair. (VICTOR *massages the back of his neck*)

ANGELINA Stiff neck?

VICTOR Yes.

ANGELINA Come here. (*He looks at her*) Come here! (VICTOR *moves to the bed*) Sit down. (*He sits facing her*) Turn around.

VICTOR What for?

ANGELINA Turn! (*He turns away. She kneels, starts to rub his neck, kneads it slowly and deliberately with both hands*) How am I doing?

VICTOR Fine.

ANGELINA Relax.

VICTOR I am relaxed. (*He allows her to continue a few moments more, then stands up*) That's much better —thanks.

ANGELINA That's all—"thanks"?

VICTOR What do you mean?

ANGELINA One good turn deserves another.

VICTOR Uh-uh.

23

ANGELINA Why?

VICTOR You know why.

ANGELINA I'm fine now.

VICTOR The doctor said eight weeks.

ANGELINA Your concern doesn't touch me.

VICTOR What's that supposed to mean?

ANGELINA You want me to say it?

VICTOR Say what?

ANGELINA I think that since there's no chance for a child, you've lost interest.

VICTOR That's ridiculous.

ANGELINA Prove it.

VICTOR Not tonight.

ANGELINA Please . . .! It's very important to me.

VICTOR I can't.

ANGELINA *Won't.*

VICTOR *Can't.*

ANGELINA Can't?

VICTOR It'll pass—just don't force me. (*She goes back to bed, turning away from him*) Good-night.
(*She doesn't reply. In the living room,* STEVE *continues to read*)

Lights down

It is afternoon, one week later.

When the lights come up, ANGELINA *is at the window overlooking the playground; she stares out raptly. The doorbell rings, and rings again before she hears it. She goes to the door and returns, accompanied by* JOSIE.

JOSIE   Steve here?

ANGELINA   No.

JOSIE   Where'd he go?

ANGELINA   I have no idea.

JOSIE   Expect him for supper?

ANGELINA   Yes.
       (JOSIE *wanders to the window overlooking the playground*)

JOSIE   There he is! (ANGELINA *regards her blankly*) Steve —he's in the playground.

ANGELINA   Oh.

JOSIE   He's playing ball—has his shirt off . . . What a body . . .

ANGELINA Josie!

JOSIE Well, he *has*. You must have noticed.

ANGELINA I've never seen him with his shirt off.

JOSIE Here's your chance.

ANGELINA I don't like that kind of talk!

JOSIE I'm sorry . . . I don't know what's the matter with me . . . Yes, I do . . . Angy. (ANGELINA *regards her*) I'm in love.

ANGELINA What?

JOSIE I love him.

ANGELINA Steve?

JOSIE Yes.

ANGELINA You hardly know him.

JOSIE Everything you're going to say, I told myself.

ANGELINA A week ago he didn't exist.

JOSIE I'm sick about him.

ANGELINA   Does he know?

JOSIE   No. Help me.

ANGELINA   Two weeks from tomorrow, he'll be gone.

JOSIE   Invite me to dinner.

ANGELINA   There's twenty fellows on the block ready to die for you. Why him?

JOSIE   After dinner, make up a reason to go out—leave us alone.

ANGELINA   Would you like me to hypnotize him?

JOSIE   Please, Angy.

ANGELINA   Put a little something in his soup?

JOSIE   Don't . . .

ANGELINA   You ought to be ashamed of yourself.

JOSIE   We all can't be like you!

ANGELINA   . . . What does *that* mean . . .? *What does that mean?*

JOSIE Some people have feelings they can't control. (ANGELINA *turns away*) I'm sorry . . . I didn't mean anything wrong . . . Angy . . .

> (*She hesitates, sees that* ANGELINA *will not respond, and then exits. We hear the door close.* ANGELINA *goes to the window overlooking the playground. She looks for an instant, and then draws the shade*)

Lights down

It is now the next morning, eleven A.M.

As the lights come up, VICTOR *stands before a mirror, knotting his tie.*

VICTOR (*To* ANGELINA, *who is offstage in the kitchen*) He gave me a great idea for fixing up the bar. (*He waits for a response from her. There is none*) It'll look better, and make more room. (*Again he waits in vain for a response*) Tell him I said he should take the day off.

   (ANGELINA, *wearing a robe, appears*)

ANGELINA How come?

VICTOR He deserves it.

ANGELINA Don't get too used to him. (VICTOR *regards her*) He leaves in two weeks.

   (VICTOR *returns his attention to the mirror and his tie*)

VICTOR He's very popular with the customers—the help, too.

ANGELINA What do you want for supper?

VICTOR I'll bring lobsters. See you later. (*He exits. We see* ZIA, *hat and coat on, emerge from her room and enter the living room*)

ZIA Want anything from Colluci's?

ANGELINA Colluci's?

ZIA I'm going to Theresa's.

ANGELINA Now?

ZIA No—yesterday . . . Well?

ANGELINA Why today?

ZIA They expect me.

ANGELINA It's so warm.

ZIA Do you want anything—yes or no?

ANGELINA Stay. We'll have lunch out . . . go to the movies.

ZIA They're expecting me.

ANGELINA Then go!

ZIA What's the matter?

ANGELINA Nothing.

ZIA You want to have lunch and go to the movies—go. What do you need *me* for?

ANGELINA You're right!
  (*She hugs* ZIA)

ZIA What's *with* you?
  (STEVE *enters*)

STEVE Good morning.

ZIA Good morning.

ANGELINA Zia, wait—I've changed my mind, I'll go with you.

ZIA I'm late now.

ANGELINA I'll only be a minute.

ZIA (*Starting to go*) I'll be home six o'clock. *Ciao.*
  (*She exits*)

ANGELINA Zia . . .!

STEVE Good morning.

ANGELINA There's coffee on the stove, juice in the refrigerator, and rolls on the table.

STEVE Thanks.

ANGELINA I'd fix it, but I'm on my way out.

32

STEVE   I'll manage. Where's Victor?

ANGELINA   He left. He said you should take the day off.

STEVE   How come?

ANGELINA   He said you earned it.

STEVE   He's right.

ANGELINA   I've got to go.
        (*She exits from the living room and reappears in
        the bedroom*)

STEVE   Where?

ANGELINA   What?

STEVE   Where are you going?

ANGELINA   . . . To the movies.
        (*She removes her robe, is wearing a slip; she
        starts to dress*)

STEVE   I've got a better idea: Let's go to the beach.

ANGELINA   . . . No.

STEVE   Why not?

33

ANGELINA   . . . I don't like the beach.

STEVE   How do you feel about Central Park?

ANGELINA   No.

STEVE   Then *you* pick a place.

ANGELINA   . . . I'm going to the movies.

STEVE   We can't talk in a movie.
(ANGELINA, *dressed, ready to leave, reappears in the living room*)

ANGELINA   Talk?

STEVE   I've been here a week—we've never talked.

ANGELINA   There's coffee on the stove—

STEVE   —Juice in the refrigerator, and rolls on the table.

ANGELINA   It's a picture I've been wanting to see.

STEVE   I understand.
(ANGELINA *starts to exit as* VICTOR *enters*)

VICTOR   I forgot the papers for Rosen. (*She goes to the bedroom to get the papers. To* STEVE) Good morning.

STEVE Good morning. I understand you're giving me the day off.

VICTOR With pay.

STEVE It's a deal.

VICTOR The Yankees are home.

STEVE I'm going to the beach.

VICTOR Every man to his own taste.

STEVE You don't like the beach either. (VICTOR *regards him questioningly*. STEVE *indicates* ANGELINA, *who returns with the papers*) I invited your wife to go. She prefers a movie.

VICTOR (*To* ANGELINA) How come? (*To* STEVE) She's crazy about the beach—always pestering me to go.

ANGELINA (*To* STEVE) I thought you were just asking to be polite. I didn't want to impose.

STEVE The offer's still open.

VICTOR Go—it'll be good for you.

ANGELINA I have shopping.

VICTOR It'll keep.

STEVE They say it'll hit ninety today.

VICTOR *Go.* You'll hurt his feelings.

ANGELINA . . . All right.

VICTOR Thatta girl. (*To* STEVE) Gotta run. (*Kisses* AN-GELINA) Have a good time.
  (*He exits. We hear the door close*)

ANGELINA While you're having breakfast, I'll get my things.

STEVE Right.

ANGELINA There's coffee on the stove—

STEVE —And juice in the refrigerator. (*For a moment they regard each other, then give way simultaneously to laughter. Abruptly* ANGELINA *stops laughing and reverts to her previous mood and manner*) The earlier we get started, the better.

STEVE Right.
  (*She goes off. He looks after her*)

Lights down

Act 1: Elena Karam as Zia and Richard Castellano as Victor.

It is now five P.M., the same day.
As the lights come up, we hear STEVE *and* ANGELINA, *returned from their day at the beach, entering the apartment.*

ANGELINA *(Offstage)* The days.

STEVE *(Offstage)* *Lunedi . . . Martedi . . . Mercoledi . . . Giovedi . . . Venerdi . . . Sabato . . . Dominica.*

ANGELINA *(Correcting him)* *Domenica.*

STEVE *Domenica.*

ANGELINA The greeting?

STEVE *Bon giorno, Signore.*

ANGELINA To a girl?

STEVE *Bon giorno, Signorina.*

ANGELINA To a pretty girl?

STEVE *(With comic leer)* *Bon giorno, Signorina.*
(They laugh)

37

ANGELINA You learn fast.

STEVE I owe it all to my teacher.
(*He flops into a chair and reacts as though in pain when his back makes contact*)

ANGELINA You really got a burn.

STEVE Is there a doctor in the house?

ANGELINA I'll see what we have.
(*She goes off. In her absence,* STEVE *gingerly removes his shirt*)

STEVE I'm glad you changed your mind.

ANGELINA (*Offstage*) What?

STEVE I'm glad you came to the beach.

ANGELINA (*Offstage*) Why?

STEVE Because I had a good time. How about you?
(ANGELINA, *bearing a tube of ointment, reappears. The sight of* STEVE *barechested, facing away, stops her. She regards him for a moment*)

ANGELINA (*Offering the tube*) Try this.

STEVE (*Accepting the tube*) Thanks.
(*As he opens the tube and begins to apply the contents, she averts her gaze*)

ANGELINA I'd like to live by it—the ocean.

STEVE Why don't you?

ANGELINA Try and get Victor to leave this neighborhood.

STEVE (*Studying her as he applies the ointment*) Why do you dress like that?

ANGELINA (*Turning to him involuntarily*) What?

STEVE You look ten years younger in a bathing suit.

ANGELINA You always say what you think?

STEVE Why not . . .? I meant it as a compliment.

ANGELINA Thanks.

STEVE You're angry.

ANGELINA Yes.

STEVE Why?

ANGELINA I don't know.

STEVE How old *are* you?

ANGELINA Thirty-six.

STEVE And Victor?

ANGELINA Why all the questions?

STEVE I'm nosey.
(*He resumes the application of the ointment*)

ANGELINA It happens every day. (STEVE *regards her*) Girls marrying older men.

STEVE How did you meet?

ANGELINA Zia raised me after my parents died. Victor went to her—said he was interested.

STEVE How old were you then?

ANGELINA Seventeen. I used to pass the restaurant— knew him to say hello. He was friendly, but I had no idea what he had in mind till Zia told me. You know what I did when she told me?

STEVE What?

ANGELINA   I laughed so hard I had a pain. (STEVE *smiles*) It's true . . . When I got through laughing, Zia warned me not to be hasty—told me what a good man he was, how well off he was, begged me to go out with him just once . . . Why not . . .? We took a ride—Zia, he, and I—brand-new Buick convertible, lunch at a fancy restaurant, anything I admired—a dog, an ashtray, a bushel of tomatoes—he wanted to buy it for me . . . It was painful. You know what I mean?

STEVE   I think so.

ANGELINA   As fas as *I* was concerned, that was the end. Not Zia. She kept at me to give him another chance. To quiet her, I said all right. He was better the second time—not so nervous, so anxious to please . . . I began to see him occasionally. In my mind, it was casual—but one step leads to another . . . The next thing you know, you see yourself in a mirror trying on a wedding gown . . . how can that be you? . . . How did it happen? (*Suddenly aware that she's been talking too much and too intimately, she stops, trying to shift the focus to* STEVE) And you? What's your story?

STEVE   Just what you know.

ANGELINA   No secrets?

STEVE   No.

ANGELINA   No girls?

STEVE No.

ANGELINA I'll bet.

STEVE Never had time.
(*He goes through futile contortions trying to apply the ointment to an area that proves unreachable*)

ANGELINA What are you doing?

STEVE There's a spot I can't reach. Can you give me a hand?
(*He offers the tube to her. She accepts it, goes behind him and starts to apply the ointment*)

ANGELINA (*As she rubs his back*) Zia was right about him—Victor. You couldn't ask for a more wonderful man, a better husband . . . There isn't a woman on the block who wouldn't change places with me.
(*Abruptly she stops applying the ointment, puts the tube down, moves away*)

ANGELINA What time is it?

STEVE (*Glancing at his watch*) Five-fifteen. How do you say *that* in Italian?

ANGELINA School is over.

STEVE . . . I see.
(*Puzzled by her behavior, he turns away and dons his shirt*)

ANGELINA What I meant is that I have things to do. (*He offers no reaction*) I *did* enjoy myself today. (*He turns to her*) If I told you how much, you'd laugh. (*She goes off*)

Lights down

It is midnight, several days later.
The lights come up on ZIA, *alone, playing cards. She hears the door open.*

ZIA Angy?

ANGELINA (*Offstage*) Yes.
  (ANGELINA *and* VICTOR *appear. He is drunk—she is angry*)

ZIA (*To* ANGELINA) How was the party? (ANGELINA *doesn't reply*) Well?

VICTOR (*To* ZIA) I'm in the doghouse.

ZIA (*To* ANGELINA) What happened?

VICTOR I made a speech.

ZIA What?

VICTOR A speech . . . *a speech!*

ZIA (*To* ANGELINA) What's he talking about?

44

ANGELINA   He stood on a chair; said he had an important announcement—told them that Steve is his son.

ZIA   *O Signore!*

ANGELINA   I prayed the floor would swallow me.

ZIA   What did they do?

VICTOR   Nothing!

ZIA   Where is he—Steve?

ANGELINA   He ran—like the place was on fire.

VICTOR   Anybody says anything ... *anything* ... they have to answer to me!

ZIA   I'm not going out tomorrow.

VICTOR   You'll go!

ZIA   (*To* ANGELINA)   He's drunk—maybe they didn't pay any attention.

ANGELINA   (*Studying* VICTOR)   He's not *that* drunk.

ZIA   Then why ... ?

ANGELINA   That's a good question.

VICTOR   One more word, I'm gonna open the window and shout it to the block!

ANGELINA (*To* ZIA)   Come on.
   (*They go off.* VICTOR, *not so drunk as he seemed previously, goes to the street window; he peers anxiously; paces; is about to look out the window again when he hears something. He waits.* STEVE *appears. They regard each other uncertainly*)

VICTOR   I was worried.

STEVE   I took a walk.

VICTOR   You left so sudden . . . I didn't mean to embarrass you.

STEVE   That wasn't it.

VICTOR   I should have asked you first.

STEVE   There's no need to apologize.

VICTOR   I don't use my head.

STEVE   I'm glad you did it . . . (VICTOR *regards him*) Really.
   (VICTOR *extends his hand.* STEVE *takes it.* VICTOR,

46

delighted and embarrassed, laughs—pumps STEVE's *hand.* STEVE, *similarly affected, also laughs. The mood spirals: They shake with mounting vigor— their laughter swells)*

Lights down

The time is several nights later.
As the lights come up, ZIA *and* ANGELINA *are sitting to-*
gether in the living room. ANGELINA *glances repeatedly at*
VICTOR *and* STEVE, *who, oblivious of* ZIA *and her, are playing*
chess.

ZIA My father, your grandfather, was a terrible spend-
thrift. Every payday he'd go on a tear—have all his
money spent before he went to bed . . .

VICTOR Check!

ZIA . . . Well, this payday he did just like usual—went
celebrating and buying drinks for everyone, from one bar
to another. By midnight he was broke. He went home,
went to bed—but he couldn't fall asleep. Kept turning
and tossing. Something was bothering him, but he didn't
know what . . .

VICTOR Did you say "resign"?

ZIA . . . Finally he couldn't stand it any more; got up,
started to get dressed, was putting on his pants when he
felt something in one of his pockets . . .

STEVE Check to *you!*

ZIA . . . He reached in—found a penny; opened the win-

48

dow, tossed the penny out into the street, went back to bed, and slept like a baby.

STEVE   Announcing mate in four.

ANGELINA   So you think I have a "penny" in my pocket?

ZIA   What?

ANGELINA   Maybe you're right.

ZIA   What's the penny got to do with *you?*

ANGELINA   *You* tell *me.*

ZIA   What are you talking about?

ANGELINA   Well, doesn't everything you say have a point, a moral?
(*The doorbell rings.* ZIA *goes to the door*)

VICTOR   I resign.

STEVE   I accept.

VICTOR   You're pretty good.

STEVE   You're not bad yourself. Another?

VICTOR   All right.
(ZIA *returns with* JOSIE, *who is trying unsuccessfully to hide her nervousness*)

JOSIE   Hi.

VICTOR   Hey—Josie.

STEVE   Hello.

JOSIE   Am I interrupting?

VICTOR   Anybody else, I'd say yes—but the prettiest girl on the block—

JOSIE   —You.

VICTOR (*To* STEVE)   She's blushing.

ANGELINA (*To* JOSIE)   What is it?

JOSIE   What?

ANGELINA   Don't you want something?

JOSIE   No.

ANGELINA   It's a social visit?

JOSIE   Yes—well, that is . . .
      (*All attention focuses on her*)

VICTOR   What is it, Josie?

JOSIE   There's going to be a dance at the Waldorf Astoria,
      Thursday night. It's for charity. All the big celebrities
      are going to be there. The tickets cost a hundred dollars
      apiece.

ZIA   We'll take fifty.

JOSIE   I'm not selling them . . .

ANGELINA   What then?

JOSIE   My boss bought two tickets, but he can't go . . .
      he gave them to *me*.

VICTOR   What time should I pick you up?

JOSIE   What?

VICTOR   Isn't that why you came—to invite me?

ANGELINA   She came to invite Steve. (*To* JOSIE) Didn't
      you?

JOSIE   . . . Yes. (*To* STEVE) Would you like to go?

51

VICTOR A hundred bucks a ticket—the Waldorf! Of course he would.

JOSIE There'll be a lot of celebrities.

VICTOR Formal?

JOSIE Yes.

VICTOR (*To* STEVE) Max'll fix you up.

ANGELINA He hasn't said he wants to go.

VICTOR Of course he wants to go. (*To* STEVE) Right?
        (STEVE *doesn't answer immediately*)

JOSIE Don't feel obligated. I mean, it was just a thought. Actually, there's someone else I should have asked. I just thought you might get a kick out of it.

STEVE I don't know how to dance.

JOSIE That doesn't matter. (STEVE *regards her uncertainly*) Really.

VICTOR It'll be mostly entertainment.

STEVE (*To* JOSIE) You're sure?

JOSIE Positive . . . Will you go?

52

STEVE   Yes.

JOSIE   Thursday—eight o'clock.

STEVE   Right.

VICTOR   And don't worry about the dancing—Josie'll teach you

STEVE   In a week?

VICTOR   What week? The dances today—a monkey could learn in five minutes. (*To* JOSIE) Show him.

JOSIE   Now?

VICTOR   Why not?
        (*He turns on the radio*)

JOSIE (*To* STEVE)   You want to?

STEVE   I don't think we have any choice.
        (VICTOR *finds a rock-and-roll number*)

VICTOR   You're on!

JOSIE (*To* STEVE)   It's simple—just do what I do.
        (*She demonstrates one of the current dances with great vigor*)

53

STEVE It's hopeless.
(*He starts away from her*)

JOSIE (*Pulling him back*) No, it isn't. It's easy. It's just this.
(*She guides him, manipulating his hips.* VICTOR *laughs*)

STEVE (*To* VICTOR) You think it's so easy, *you* try it.
(JOSIE *goes to* VICTOR *with the intention of getting him to dance*)

JOSIE Come on.

VICTOR (*Waving her away*) I'll get my own partner.
(JOSIE *returns to* STEVE *and resumes teaching him.* VICTOR *beckons* ANGELINA *to dance with him. She refuses. He goes to* ZIA)

VICTOR Come on.

ZIA No.

VICTOR Come on!
(*He gives* ZIA *no choice; he pulls her to her feet and compels her to dance*)

ZIA You crazy thing!

VICTOR (*To* JOSIE *and* STEVE) We challenge you.

54

STEVE   We accept.

JOSIE (*To* VICTOR *and* ZIA *as she breaks into a new step*)
Try this.
> (VICTOR *and* ZIA *try to emulate the kids. A happy
> mood spirals until* ANGELINA, *unable to bear what
> is happening, snaps the radio off. They all regard
> her curiously*)

ANGELINA (*Trying to make light of what she's done*)
Have you lost your minds? . . . It's late. (*They continue
to regard her*) I hate that music!
> (*She hastens to the bedroom*)

ZIA (*To the others*)   Stay.
> (*She follows* ANGELINA *off*)

JOSIE   I think I better go.

VICTOR   You were doing fine—don't stop.
> (JOSIE *regards* STEVE *uncertainly*)

STEVE   I could use another lesson.
> (VICTOR *turns the radio on and locates a foxtrot,
> slow and dreamy*)

VICTOR   Try that.
> (*As* JOSIE *starts to teach* STEVE *this step,* VICTOR
> *turns from them and directs his attention toward
> the bedroom, where* ZIA *is confronting* ANGELINA)

ZIA   *Che cosa è? Che succede?*

ANGELINA   I have a headache.

ZIA   I don't mean tonight.

ANGELINA   I don't know what you're talking about.

ZIA   Victor don't see—but I see: You haven't been yourself for weeks.

ANGELINA   Do me a favor—leave me alone!

ZIA   Will you go to the doctor?

ANGELINA   For what?

ZIA   For me.

ANGELINA   . . . All right.

ZIA   Tomorrow.

ANGELINA   All right.

ZIA   You'll take a warm bath now—go to bed.
      (*In the living room* JOSIE *emits a burst of laughter as she and* STEVE *dance.* ANGELINA *breaks down; she lays her head in* ZIA's *lap and weeps.* ZIA *cradles her*)

56

ZIA What's the matter . . . ? What is it . . . ?
(JOSIE *laughs again*)

Curtain

Act Two

The time is eight P.M., *the night of the dance.*
As the curtain rises, ZIA *sits in an attitude of imminent*
departure. ANGELINA, *preoccupied, fans herself.* VICTOR
moves about impatiently.

VICTOR   What's taking them so long?

ZIA   She's a girl.

VICTOR   He promised they'd stop in.

ZIA *(To* ANGELINA*)*   Remember how long you used to
take?

VICTOR   Maybe he forgot—maybe they went.

ANGELINA   Suppose they did. What's the tragedy?

ZIA *(To* VICTOR*)*   What time *is* it?

VICTOR *(Checking his watch)*   Five after eight.

ZIA   I can't wait any more.

VICTOR   I'm going to see what's what.
        (He goes off. ZIA *rises)*

ZIA (*To* ANGELINA)   It's all right if I go?

ANGELINA   What do I care?

ZIA   You won't come?

ANGELINA   No.

ZIA   Saint Jude's been good to you.

ANGELINA   Please!

ZIA   I won't say another word.

ANGELINA   Thank you.
        (ZIA *puts on her hat—turns to* ANGELINA)

ZIA   I'm going.

ANGELINA   All right!

ZIA   . . . It might be just what you need.

ANGELINA   All I need is for the summer to be over.

ZIA   . . . Those pills are in your nightstand.

ANGELINA   I know!

ZIA A good night's sleep wouldn't do you any harm . . .
I won't be late.
(ZIA *exits. A moment later,* VICTOR *returns*)

VICTOR She had to have a hem fixed—they'll be right
down. (*He resumes his fitful movement about the room;
he goes to the window fronting the street and gazes
down*) I was figuring the other day that if I had sup-
ported him all these years, it would have cost twenty-five
thousand dollars. (*Turns to* ANGELINA) At least twenty-
five.

ANGELINA So what?

VICTOR It's something to keep in mind.

ANGELINA Why?
(*The bell rings. He goes off and reappears a few
moments later. He poses in the living-room entrance*)

VICTOR Announcing the arrival of the prince and the
princess. (*He steps aside.* STEVE *and* JOSIE, *in formal
attire, their youth and beauty breathtaking to behold,
enter. To* ANGELINA) Are *they* something? (*To* STEVE
and JOSIE) In my whole life, I've never seen a prettier-
looking . .
(*Overwhelmed, he is unable to continue*)

STEVE Hey.

VICTOR Sorry

JOSIE (*Revolving to show the gown to* ANGELINA) You really like it?

ANGELINA Yes.

JOSIE Where's Zia?

ANGELINA Novena.

VICTOR I wish I had a camera.

JOSIE (*To* STEVE) We better get started.

STEVE. Yes.

VICTOR How you going?

STEVE Cab.

VICTOR I got a better idea. Come here. (*He moves to the window overlooking the street.* STEVE *and* JOSIE *follow him. He is pointing*) See there—that white car—the convertible?

STEVE Yes.

VICTOR Here. (*He holds out a set of car keys to* STEVE) The registration's in the glove compartment.

JOSIE Whose is it?

64

VICTOR   Steve's.

STEVE   *What?*

VICTOR   If you don't like the color or the model, you can have it changed.

STEVE   (*To* ANGELINA)   What's he talking about?

ANGELINA   Offhand, I'd say he's giving you a car.
         (STEVE *regards* VICTOR *incredulously*)

VICTOR   Go.

STEVE   *Why?*

VICTOR   Don't ask dumb questions.

STEVE   But—

VICTOR   —The dance already started.

STEVE   My head's spinning.

VICTOR   I'll be your first passenger. You can drop me at the restaurant.

STEVE   At least let me say thank you.

VICTOR   You're welcome—let's go.

65

STEVE (*To* ANGELINA) And thank *you.*

ANGELINA I had nothing to do with it.

VICTOR (*To* STEVE) Come on.
(JOSIE *dashes over to* ANGELINA—*kisses her warmly*)

JOSIE This is the happiest night of my life.

VICTOR Let's go!

STEVE (*To* ANGELINA) Good-night.

JOSIE (*To* ANGELINA) Good-night.

VICTOR Don't wait up
(*They exit.* ANGELINA *remains as she is for a moment, goes to the window and looks down. She then turns back into the room, goes to a sideboard bearing a wine decanter and glasses and pours a glass of wine. She is drinking the wine when her attention is arrested by her reflection in the mirror above the sideboard. She regards herself; she lets her hair down. She then moves closer to the mirror and becomes lost in contemplation of herself*)

Lights down

It is now three hours later.

As the lights come up, ANGELINA, *in her slip, reclines on the sofa. The apartment is in darkness until* ZIA *enters, turns on a light, discovers* ANGELINA. *She then notes the half-filled wine decanter and empty glass on the table beside her.*

ZIA   Angy . . . Angy, what do you call this?

ANGELINA (*Regarding* ZIA *with drunken amusement*) How's Saint Jude?

ZIA   *What?*

ANGELINA   Poor Zia.

ZIA   Get up.

ANGELINA (*Sings loudly*)   "Vidi na croce su questu canone . . . Muriva senza suono di campane . . ."

ZIA   Go to bed—we'll talk in the morning.

ANGELINA   Nothing serious he said—just nerves.

ZIA (*Trying to help her up*)   Come.

67

ANGELINA   What killed her? Nothing serious—just nerves.
   (*She laughs*)

ZIA (*Attempting unsuccessfully to get her to her feet*)   I
   can't do it alone.

ANGELINA (*Pushing her away—savagely*)   You've done
   enough!
      (ANGELINA *gets up on her own. She takes her wine
      glass and wanders about*)

ZIA   Are you trying to frighten me?

ANGELINA   Poor Zia . . . Tell me something, poor Zia: did
   I advertise? Did I go looking for him?

ZIA   For who?

ANGELINA   A punishment? For what?

ZIA   I don't understand.

ANGELINA   Did I ever look at another man?

ZIA   What are you talking about?

ANGELINA   *Did I ever look at another man?*
      (ZIA *regards her—says nothing*)

68

ANGELINA (*Screams*) *Answer me!*

ZIA (*Hastily closing the window*) You want the police?
(ANGELINA *laughs at her*)

ANGELINA Not once . . . *not once.*
(ZIA, *sensing real trouble, moves to* ANGELINA)

ZIA (*Probing*) What?

ANGELINA (*Moving away from her and to the window*)
"*Vidi na croce su questu canone* . . ."

ZIA Who?

ANGELINA (*Looking out the window*) It hurt my eyes to
look at him the first time—like he was the sun. (*Turns to*
ZIA) And he is.
(*She laughs*)

ZIA (*Explosively*) Who?

ANGELINA It took everything I had not to follow him, and
then Victor brought him here.
(*Laughing,* ANGELINA *goes into the bedroom—sits
on the bed.* ZIA, *horrified by what she's learned, takes
a moment to collect herself, then follows*)

ZIA Listen to me.

ANGELINA A punishment? For what?

69

ZIA Listen! (*She gains* ANGELINA's *attention*) *Has he touched you?*

ANGELINA No.

ZIA Does he know how you feel?

ANGELINA No.

ZIA Then it will be all right.

ANGELINA What did she die of? Nothing serious. Just nerves.

ZIA He's leaving in a week!

ANGELINA A week?

ZIA The thirtieth—a week from yesterday.

ANGELINA (*Softly, almost to herself*) "*Vidi na croce su questu canone . . .*"

ZIA Less than a week.

ANGELINA ". . . *Muriva senza suono di campane . . .*"

Lights down

It is the next morning.
The lights come up on ANGELINA, *asleep in the bedroom.*
ZIA, *alone in the living room, is packing the tuxedo* STEVE
wore. VICTOR, *a cup of coffee in his hand, enters.*

VICTOR   I'll drop it off. He didn't get in till three.

ZIA   You waited up?

VICTOR   Yes . . . Angy's still asleep.

ZIA   She was very tired.

VICTOR   I have some news.

ZIA   What?

VICTOR   I want her to hear first . . . I'm going to wake her.

ZIA   No!

VICTOR   I've got to go.

ZIA   . . . I'll get her.
        (*She goes off.* VICTOR *sits down. He picks up a*
        newspaper, drinks his coffee and reads. ZIA *enters*

71

the bedroom; she raises the shades. The light rouses
ANGELINA)

ANGELINA   Hey!

ZIA   It's after ten.

ANGELINA   Go away.

ZIA   Victor wants to talk to you.

ANGELINA   ... What is it?

ZIA   I don't know.

ANGELINA   *You* put me to bed?

ZIA   Yes.

ANGELINA   I drank too much.

ZIA   No kidding.

ANGELINA   I think I carried on.

ZIA   Yes.

ANGELINA   Talked a lot.

72

ZIA   Yes.

ANGELINA   About what?

ZIA   Who could tell?

ANGELINA   It didn't make sense?

ZIA   Not to me.

ANGELINA   Not a word?

ZIA   Not a word

ANGELINA   I never did that before—got drunk!

ZIA   Victor's waiting. (ANGELINA *gets out of bed.* ZIA *is helping her on with her robe.* ANGELINA *hesitates*) The other arm.

ANGELINA   You don't know what he wants?

ZIA   No.

ANGELINA   Does he know I was drunk?

ZIA   No.

73

ANGELINA Maybe I talked in my sleep—said something that upset him.

ZIA Once you got in bed, you were dead to the world.

ANGELINA Does he look upset?

ZIA No . . . Come.
(ANGELINA *follows* ZIA *into the living room*)

VICTOR Good morning.

ANGELINA 'Morning.

VICTOR Sorry to wake you.

ANGELINA That's all right . . . Zia said you have something to tell me.

VICTOR Yes . . .

ANGELINA What is it?

VICTOR I waited up for Steve . . . We talked . . .

ANGELINA And?

VICTOR He's staying.

ANGELINA What?

VICTOR He's not going back.

ZIA (*To* VICTOR) What are you talking about?

VICTOR (*To* ZIA) Steve's going to live here—in New York. (*He looks to* ANGELINA *for a reaction. She offers none*) Well? (*She just looks at him*) What do you say? (*She continues to look at him*) You don't like it. (*No reaction*) Why not? (*No reaction*) Once he gets the hang of the restaurant, you and I can take vacations—travel. (*Still no reaction*) What have you got against him? (*Still no reaction*) He's the only son I'll ever have!

ANGELINA If you love him, send him away.

VICTOR Why? (*She starts from the room*) He's staying!

ANGELINA (*She stops and turns to him*) I saw the look on your face when you came to the hospital: You wanted to be rid of me so someone else could give you children.

VICTOR No.

ANGELINA You wished me dead. (VICTOR *is unable to respond*) The tickets for the dance: *you* got them—not her boss.
  (*She exits to the bedroom*)

75

VICTOR (*To* ZIA)   What's the matter with her?

ZIA   The house is on fire—where are *you*?
  (*She hands* VICTOR *the tuxedo. He regards her a
  moment, then exits from the house.* ZIA *goes to the
  bedroom.* ANGELINA, *who has been contemplating
  a vial of pills, pockets them guiltily as* ZIA *enters*)

ANGELINA   Get out.

ZIA   What are you doing?

ANGELINA   Get out!

ZIA   What have you got there?

ANGELINA   Nothing.

ZIA (*Reaching for* ANGELINA's *pocket*)   What have you
  got there?

ANGELINA   *Lasciamme!*

ZIA   *Che cos'è?*

ANGELINA   You really want to know?
  (*Taking the vial from her pocket, she thrusts it at*
  ZIA)

ZIA (*Taking the vial—regarding it*) These are . . . What for . . . ? (*Now the monstrous implication hits her. She regards* ANGELINA) You fool! . . . *You fool!*

ANGELINA If you knew.

ZIA How it hurt your eyes to look at him in the playground? (ANGELINA *regards her incredulously*) Yes!

ANGELINA Everything?

ZIA What "everything"? You got a crush.

ANGELINA Don't.

ZIA Nothing happened—you told me yourself.

ANGELINA Stop!

ZIA Something *did* happen.

ANGELINA No!

ZIA (*Indicating the pills*) Then why?

ANGELINA After, it will be too late.

ZIA He'll be out of the house tonight—I guarantee!

77

ANGELINA   I wouldn't have the will.

ZIA   You'll never seen him again!

ANGELINA   I think *that* would kill me too.

ZIA   (*Commandingly*) Look at me! (ANGELINA *regards her.* ZIA *indicates the vial*) *This* is a worse sin than the other.

ANGELINA   And it's better to bend than to break.

ZIA   Yes.

ANGELINA   No!

ZIA   So all lovers have to die.

ANGELINA   (*Shocked*) *You* say that? *You,* who helped to crucify Mrs. Alvarez?

ZIA   You want to blame someone—blame *me!*

ANGELINA   Now what?

ZIA   *I* made you marry Victor. Put it on *my* head.

ANGELINA   Of course.

78

ZIA   And what would happen to *him*—Victor?

ANGELINA (*Savagely*)   You would take care of him—just like you always dreamed! (ZIA *slaps her hard across the face. For a moment, equally shocked and regretful, they regard each other*) I'm so sorry.

ZIA   Give me time.

ANGELINA   For what?

ZIA   I'll think of something . . . Have I ever failed you . . . ? Give me time . . . All right?

ANGELINA   . . . All right.

ZIA   Lie down now—rest—trust me.
    (*She starts from the room, bearing the vial of pills*)

ANGELINA   Leave them. (ZIA *hesitates*) Trust me.
    (ZIA *puts the vial on a nightstand, then exits.* ANGELINA *returns to bed.* ZIA *enters the living room. The desperate feelings she suppressed in* ANGELINA'S *presence are apparent now as she searches for a solution.* STEVE *enters the living room*)

STEVE   Zia—the tuxedo, did Victor take it? (*She nods almost imperceptibly.* STEVE *regards her more closely— senses something wrong*) You all right? (*She offers no reaction*) What is it? What's the matter?

79

ZIA Angelina . . .

STEVE What's wrong . . . ? Well?

ZIA She won't say.

STEVE You mean sick?

ZIA No.

STEVE Then what?

ZIA I don't know.

STEVE Anything I can do?
(*This question spawns a thought in* ZIA's *mind. She rises and faces* STEVE)

ZIA Yes . . .

STEVE Name it . . . Well?

ZIA Talk to her—find out what's the matter.

STEVE Me?

ZIA She likes you, trusts you. (STEVE *regards her skeptically*) She told me so . . . Will you do it?

STEVE Talk to her?

ZIA Yes.

STEVE About what?

ZIA You noticed she hasn't been herself: Is there anything wrong? . . . can you help? . . . (*To* STEVE *directly*) All right?

STEVE I don't know.

ZIA You don't care about her.

STEVE Of course I do.

ZIA She's in her room.

STEVE You mean, now?

ZIA Yes . . . Please.

STEVE You're really worried. (ZIA *nods*) Just talk to her and . . . (ZIA *nods*) She might resent it. (ZIA's *look tells that any further protest is futile*) Her room?

ZIA Yes. (*He exhales resignedly, braces himself and starts from the room*) One thing. (*He turns to her*) Your word you won't say anything about this to anyone.

STEVE Wild horses couldn't drag it out of me.

ZIA It's not a joke!

STEVE Sorry.
(*She turns away. He regards her an instant, then goes off.* ZIA *sits. There is a knock at the bedroom door. Silence. Another knock.* ANGELINA *stirs*)

ANGELINA What?

STEVE (*Outside her bedroom door*) It's me—Steve. (ANGELINA, *instantly alert, sits up*) Angelina? . . . Angelina?

ANGELINA . . . What do you want?

STEVE (*Still outside*) I'd like to talk to you. (*No response*) Angelina?

ANGELINA . . . It's open.

STEVE (*Still outside*) What?

ANGELINA The door's open.
(*He enters the shadowed room tentatively*)

STEVE Good morning. (*She studies him*) I woke you. (*She continues to regard him*) It can wait till later.

ANGELINA Close it. (*He closes the door and turns to her; he hesitates*) You're embarrassed.

82

STEVE Yes.

ANGELINA I'm glad.

STEVE Why?

ANGELINA Excuse the way I look.

STEVE You look fine. How do you feel?

ANGELINA Like in a dream—like nothing's real.

STEVE What's wrong?

ANGELINA Maybe it is. (*He regards her uncomprehendingly*) A dream—maybe it is, huh?

STEVE Maybe.

ANGELINA . . . You wanted to talk to me.

STEVE Yes . . .

ANGELINA Go on.

STEVE You haven't been yourself lately. I thought maybe there was something wrong, something you might like to tell me . . . Well?

ANGELINA If I asked you to leave and never come back—
would you do it?

STEVE What?

ANGELINA If I asked you to leave this house, right now,
and never come back—would you do it?

STEVE Why?

ANGELINA *Would you do it?*

STEVE If I thought you really wanted me to . . . Do you?
. . . Well? (*She begins to cry. He goes to her, sits on
the bed, takes her hand*) What is it? . . . What is it?

ANGELINA You came here—I didn't go to you. (*She looks
to him for confirmation*) *You* came to *me*.

STEVE That's right. (*She kisses his hand*) Angy—what
is it . . . ? Tell me . . . I want to help.
    (*She kisses him on the mouth. A moment of deep
    contact, then* STEVE *recoils; he would pull away, but
    she holds him fast. With a violent jerk he breaks
    her grip, rises, and then backs away*)

ANGELINA What's the matter? (*He just looks at her*)
What is it? (*Expression unchanged, he continues to regard her*) You never kissed a girl before? (*Still no response*) What? (*She gets out of bed; she studies him.
The truth begins to occur to her*) Why did you come
here? . . . For what?

STEVE   Zia said something was wrong.

ANGELINA   Zia—of course . . . That's very funny . . . Don't you see? . . . Look at the face on him . . . ! Say it!

STEVE   What is there to say?

ANGELINA   I love you.

STEVE   Get off it.

ANGELINA   What do I do now?

STEVE   Go back to the playground—get yourself another boy.

ANGELINA   (*Turns from him as though struck*) . . . Yes . . . Of course.

STEVE   (*Realizing how deeply he's hurt her, he is regretful*) I'm sorry.

ANGELINA   Get out. (*He just stands there. She screams*) *Get out!*
        (*He exits and enters the living room; he now confronts* ZIA)

STEVE   You bitch . . . You dirty old bitch . . . You knew what would happen—didn't you . . . ? *Didn't you?*

85

ZIA Yes . . . and so did *you*.
(*He regards her an instant; then he exits from the apartment. In the bedroom,* ANGELINA *sits on the edge of the bed*)

ANGELINA (*Coldly, bitterly*) I've been here a week—we haven't talked." . . . "You look ten years younger in a bathing suit." . . . "Rub my back."
(*She removes the crucifix from about her neck; she removes her wedding ring; she places both of them on the pillow and then freezes*)

Lights down

It is now late that night.

When the lights come up the apartment is in darkness,
except for the light coming in from the street.

VICTOR, *barely discernible, preferably unnoticed, sits*
alone in the living room.

The sound of the front door opening is heard. STEVE
enters the living room, turns on a lamp; he is startled to
discover VICTOR *who, expression glazed, regards him as*
though he were an apparition.

STEVE (*Tapping his heart*) Hey—what are you trying
to do to me . . . ? (VICTOR, *expression unchanged, con-*
tinues to regard him) What's up—what are you sitting
in the dark for . . . ? (*No response*) You all right . . . ?
(*No response*) Matter of fact, I'm glad you're up. I was
going to speak to you in the morning—I'll do it now . . .
(*Still no response.* STEVE, *increasingly uneasy, moves*
about to avoid VICTOR's *gaze*) I don't know exactly how
to put it, but I've been doing a lot of thinking, and I've
come to a decision: I'm going to leave, go back out West
—at least till I finish school . . . (*Forces himself to face*
VICTOR) You understand, I like it here—can't remember
a better time, or when people were nicer to me—espe-
cially you . . . (*Still no reaction from* VICTOR. STEVE *turns*
away) I figure I should look around a bit, learn more,
before I settle down . . . I know this is a lot to spring on
you all of a sudden, and I apologize for not saying anything sooner . . . (*No response.* STEVE *regards him*) Well,
what do you say? . . . (*No response, no reaction*) What's
wrong with you? . . . Something the matter . . . ? *What*

87

is it . . . ? (*He still gets no response.* STEVE, *fighting to retain control of himself, turns away*) Look—I don't know what's bothering you, but I—(STEVE's *movement has brought him to the rear of a chair over which* VICTOR's *suit jacket is draped. Something he sees arrests his attention. He stops, stares, looks from the jacket to* VICTOR, *and back again. He then slowly reaches for the jacket and lifts it to expose a mourning band on the left sleeve; he regards it*) What's this for? . . . Why? . . . For who? (*As though it were suddenly hot to the touch,* STEVE *drops the jacket; he turns to* VICTOR, *exercising great control*) Where's Angelina? (VICTOR *remains unchanged*) I want to speak to her. (*No reaction*) Wake her up. (*No reaction*) If you don't—I will!

(*Still no reaction.* STEVE *rushes to the bedroom. He turns on the light. The bed is stripped. A crucifix on the wall above the bed is draped in black. An unmistakably funereal air pervades the room. He snaps the light off—returns to the living room*)

STEVE   How? . . . An accident . . . ? What? . . . Say something! (VICTOR *takes a letter from his pocket; he proffers it.* STEVE *hesitates a moment, moves to* VICTOR, *takes the letter. He reads it and regards* VICTOR *incredulously*) It's not so—not any of it.

VICTOR   She lied?

STEVE   Yes.

VICTOR   Why?

88

STEVE I don't know.

VICTOR Maybe she was disturbed—unbalanced?

STEVE I don't know.

VICTOR Hated the son she could never give me?

STEVE I don't know.

VICTOR Took her life to spite you?

STEVE I could have had lots of girls. Why *her*?

VICTOR A bastard's revenge.

STEVE For what? You loved me, acknowledged me.

VICTOR How long did you plan it?

STEVE Don't!

VICTOR How long did you watch the house?

STEVE Stop!

VICTOR You're shouting. Why? You can't outshout what's
written there.
     (STEVE, *searching desperately for a way to rebut the
     charge, goes to* ZIA's *closed door*)

89

STEVE   Zia? (*No answer. He knocks*) Zia! (*No answer. He tries the handle, but finds the door locked; he beats on it*) Zia—Zia, please? (*Still no answer.* VICTOR *rises; he faces* STEVE *as he re-enters the living room*)

VICTOR   Get out! (STEVE *weeps*) Tears . . .? What for? . . . You shouldn't have any trouble finding another house where you can sneak into the husband's heart— the wife's bed.

STEVE   Stop! For your *own* sake!

VICTOR   My sake?

STEVE   I beg you.

VICTOR   *Before* you took her—*that* was the time for "my sake."

STEVE   If you really believe that, why don't you kill me? . . . Go on!

VICTOR   It wants more than that.
        (STEVE *regards* VICTOR *with vaulting horror; he dashes out.* VICTOR *remains as he is.* ZIA *emerges from her room*)

ZIA   He's gone?

VICTOR   Yes.

ZIA   . . . Can I get you something?

VICTOR   I showed him the letter. He swore it wasn't so.

ZIA   What did you expect?

VICTOR   Was I too quick?

ZIA   He's guilty!

VICTOR   Then why do I have this feeling, this doubt?

ZIA   You're tired.

VICTOR   He said—

ZIA   (*In an outburst*) —*Who cares what he said?* (*This outburst draws* VICTOR's *attention. He regards* ZIA. *His scrutiny unsettles her. She becomes increasingly agitated*) Said what . . .? Whatever he said, there's nothing to it . . . Want some tea? I'll make you some . . . In his condition he'd accuse anyone. Why not? What has he got to lose? . . . What's the matter? Why're you looking like that . . .? I'll bet he even brought me into it—huh? . . . Sure . . . All right, what did he say about me?

VICTOR   Nothing—not a word.

ZIA   Then why are you looking like that?

VICTOR You're so nervous.

ZIA The blackest day of my life—who wouldn't be?

VICTOR Trembling.

ZIA I'm going back to bed.

VICTOR Why didn't you come out when he called?

ZIA I was asleep.

VICTOR How did you know he was here?

ZIA We'll talk in the morning.

VICTOR Why didn't you come out when he called?

ZIA I didn't want to see him.

VICTOR Miss a chance to accuse, to punish? *You? (She would escape to her room—he blocks the way)* Tell me.

ZIA Let me go.

VICTOR Tell me!

ZIA I feel faint.

92

VICTOR Tell me!

ZIA She loved him! (VICTOR *regards her incredulously*)
Yes. (VICTOR *turns away*) She was dying for him, and
he had no idea. Could I just let her die? Do nothing . . .?
I made up a reason—sent him to her . . . When he
realized what it was all about, he walked out.

VICTOR Nothing happened?

ZIA Nothing—everything: What's it matter now?
    (*They are interrupted by the sound of* JOSIE, *who
    bursts into the apartment crying hysterically*)

JOSIE *Victor! Victor!*

VICTOR What is it?
    (*She grabs him, pulls him toward the door*)

JOSIE Come with me . . .? Please come with me!
    (VICTOR *grips her, immobilizes her*)

VICTOR What's the matter?

JOSIE (*Numbly*) He got in the car—raced off. I saw him
turn the corner. I heard a crash . . . so loud.

VICTOR He's hurt?

93

JOSIE He's dying. (VICTOR *dashes out*) Nothing will ever be so wonderful again . . . Nothing.

Lights down

*The setting is the playground, the same as in Scene 1,
Act One*
The time is the immediate continuation of the last scene.
*As the lights come up the playground is in darkness,
except for light from a street lamp.* STEVE *lies in the circle
of light.* VICTOR *kneels behind him.*

VICTOR (*To the audience as though they were a crowd of
onlookers*) Keep off! . . . *Keep off!*

STEVE   Father?

VICTOR   Yes?

STEVE   I can't see.

VICTOR   The light's gone out.

STEVE   Father?

VICTOR   Yes?

STEVE   My legs are numb.

VICTOR   The summer's over—there's a chill in the air.

STEVE   Father?

VICTOR Yes?

STEVE Hold me. Raise me up.

VICTOR To heaven, if I could.

Curtain

Far Rockaway

FAR ROCKAWAY *was first presented on National Educational Television under the auspices of the Lincoln Center in September, 1965, with the following cast:*

(In order of appearance)

MICHAEL ST. JOHN	Michael Higgins
MRS. ST. JOHN	Frances Sternhagen
THE NEIGHBOR	Kay Medford
HIS EMPLOYER	Milo Boulton
DR. WALGREEN	Kermit Murdock
DESK SERGEANT	Moses Gunn
THE PRIEST	John Heffernan
MRS. BROWN	Ann Wedgeworth
FIRST GRAVEDIGGER	Tom Pedi
SECOND GRAVEDIGGER	Lou Gilbert

Directed by Ulu Grosbard
Staged for television by Kirk Browning
Settings by Ed Wittstein
Produced by Jac Venza

Act 2: Jon Voight as Steve, Irene Papas as Angelina
Capuano.

MICHAEL ST. JOHN (*Reading the inscription on a plaque*) "On January fifth, at eleven A.M., Michael St. John, while strolling the beach at Far Rockaway, did kill a fleeing murderer."

MRS. ST. JOHN   I still don't know what he was doing at Far Rockaway at eleven A.M. on a Monday.

MICHAEL ST. JOHN (*from the plaque*) ". . . is hereby awarded this plaque for valor in the public interest."

MRS. ST. JOHN   I was doing my nails when my neighbor burst in.

THE NEIGHBOR   Michael killed a murderer at Far Rockaway. It just came over the radio.

MRS. ST. JOHN   Don't be absurd.

THE NEIGHBOR   Michael St. John.

MRS. ST. JOHN   I know my husband.

THE NEIGHBOR   Thirty-eight. Civil engineer.

MRS. ST. JOHN   Wouldn't harm a fly.

THE NEIGHBOR   This address.

MRS. ST. JOHN   What would Michael be doing at Far Rockaway at eleven A.M. on a Monday?

THE NEIGHBOR   She's got a point.

MICHAEL ST. JOHN   Ate my usual breakfast that morning. Left the house at the usual time.

MRS. ST. JOHN   Pecked me on the cheek as usual.

MICHAEL ST. JOHN   My subway pulled into the station. The doors opened . . .

THE NEIGHBOR (*Reading from a newspaper*)   "The next thing I knew," said Mr. St. John, "I was standing on the beach at Far Rockaway, gun in hand, this fellow dead at my feet."

MRS. ST. JOHN   Far Rockaway at eleven A.M. on a Monday? I don't understand.

MICHAEL ST. JOHN   Neither do I.

THE NEIGHBOR (*From the newspaper*)   "Mr. St. John suffered a partial amnesia induced by the . . . continued on page forty-eight."

HIS EMPLOYER   I've always been a good judge of men, but St. John—Mike, that is—fooled me. Been with my firm twelve years. Honest, competent, decent—but you'd never take him for a hero. Yes, I was really fooled by St. John—Mike, that is.

THE NEIGHBOR They'd been trying to have children for a long time. Had given up, in fact.

MRS. ST. JOHN There was blood on his cuff . . . a strange odor about him.

THE NEIGHBOR She conceived that night.

HIS EMPLOYER Mind if I call you "Mike"?

MICHAEL ST. JOHN The neighborhood kids stopped letting the air out of my tires.

THE NEIGHBOR In a word—he prospered.

HIS EMPLOYER   Just between us, Mike—what's it like to kill a man?

MICHAEL ST. JOHN   Sad.

THE NEIGHBOR   Could Gary Cooper put it better?

HIS EMPLOYER   I made him Chief of Sales.

MICHAEL ST. JOHN   I began to have nightmares.

THE NEIGHBOR   Some people can't stand prosperity.

MICHAEL ST. JOHN Oh, my God.

THE NEIGHBOR (*Reading from a newspaper*) "Mr. St. John's amnesia is of a temporary nature," said Doctor P. H. Walgreen, psychiatrist. "In short . . ."

DR. WALGREEN . . . he'll remember everything that happened, someday.

MICHAEL ST. JOHN *Oh, my God!*

DR. WALGREEN What did I tell you?

MICHAEL ST. JOHN   I'm not a hero.

MRS. ST. JOHN   The neighbors are sure we'll have a boy.

MICHAEL ST. JOHN   I didn't have to shoot that fellow.

MRS. ST. JOHN   It's very active just now—feel.

MICHAEL ST. JOHN   He'd broken his ankle—was lying helpless on the beach.

MRS. ST. JOHN   How cold your hand is.

MICHAEL ST. JOHN   He reached up—gave me his gun.

MRS. ST. JOHN   What shall we call it if it's a boy?

MICHAEL ST. JOHN   Je-*sus*!

MRS. ST. JOHN   And if it's a girl?

MICHAEL ST. JOHN   I didn't *kill him* . . . I *murdered* him.

MRS. ST. JOHN   You haven't heard a word I said.

SCENE 6

MICHAEL ST. JOHN   I didn't have to shoot that fellow.

HIS EMPLOYER   Your tie is stained.

MICHAEL ST. JOHN   He'd broken his leg.

HIS EMPLOYER   You need a haircut.

MICHAEL ST. JOHN   Handed me his gun . . .

HIS EMPLOYER   And a shine . . .

MICHAEL ST. JOHN   *I murdered him.*

HIS EMPLOYER   Something wrong, Mike?

MICHAEL ST. JOHN   I want to report a murder.

DESK SERGEANT   The same one you reported yesterday?

MICHAEL ST. JOHN   I didn't have to kill him.

DESK SERGEANT   We've been over that.

MICHAEL ST. JOHN   Arrest me.

DESK SERGEANT   The law is satisfied.

MICHAEL ST. JOHN   Arrest me!

DESK SERGEANT   There's no complaint.

MICHAEL ST. JOHN   There's a body.

DESK SERGEANT   It's been accounted for.

MICHAEL ST. JOHN   But—

DESK SERGEANT   —It's been accounted for!

DR. WALGREEN To demand a penalty of yourself that society doesn't require is neurotic.

MICHAEL ST. JOHN I like the sound of that.

DR. WALGREEN We must find out who you killed that morning at Far Rockaway.

MICHAEL ST. JOHN A fellow named Brown.

DR. WALGREEN We must discover your victim's name.

MICHAEL ST. JOHN William Brown—it was in the papers.

DR. WALGREEN We must learn for whom those bullets were *really* intended.

MICHAEL ST. JOHN William Brown!

DR. WALGREEN Shall we begin?
    (HOWARD *exits, slamming the door*)

SCENE 9

MICHAEL ST. JOHN   I've killed a man.

THE PRIEST   The confidences of the confessional are inviolate.

MICHAEL ST. JOHN   Can it be forgiven?

THE PRIEST   If it's repented.

MICHAEL ST. JOHN   Would I be here if I wasn't sorry?

THE PRIEST   Given the chance, would you do it again?

MICHAEL ST. JOHN   I want to say no—but it sticks in my throat.

MICHAEL ST. JOHN I killed your husband.

MRS. BROWN Please come in.

MICHAEL ST. JOHN He was lying on the beach.

MRS. BROWN Do you know how many men he killed?

MICHAEL ST. JOHN His leg was broken.

MRS. BROWN He raped his sister when she was eight.

MICHAEL ST. JOHN Handed me his gun.

MRS. BROWN Beat the children, so that one is crippled.

MICHAEL ST. JOHN Two bullets in his heart—one in his head.

MRS. BROWN God bless you.

MICHAEL ST. JOHN I *murdered* him.

MRS. BROWN Will you stay for tea?

MRS. ST. JOHN I needed butter—was phoning Michael at the office to bring some home, when my neighbor came in.

THE NEIGHBOR I just passed Michael running down the street.

MRS. ST. JOHN (*On the phone*) May I speak to Mr. St. John, please . . .?

THE NEIGHBOR "Where's the fire?" I shouted.

MRS. ST. JOHN (*Still on the phone*) There must be some mistake . . .

THE NEIGHBOR "Far Rockaway," he shouted back. "A terrible blaze."

MRS. ST. JOHN (*Putting down the phone*) They say Michael hasn't been at the office in a week.

THE NEIGHBOR Did you hear anything about a fire at Far Rockaway?

MICHAEL ST. JOHN (*He shivers*)   The water's colder than
it looked.

SCENE 13

FIRST GRAVEDIGGER   I heard it was suicide.

SECOND GRAVEDIGGER   There was talk.

FIRST GRAVEDIGGER   How is he buried in church ground?

SECOND GRAVEDIGGER   They stretch a point for heroes.

Blackout